Praise for Honor: The Signet of The Prophetic Voice

"The author Janice Watts supplies an in-depth analysis of various aspects of Honor often glossed over in other books. Some of the areas explored include the effects of dishonor. " The spirit of Dishonor comes to rob you of what you have been assigned ruler-ship over." Along with solid biblical teaching, I was taken on a journey of spiritual, emotional and practical wisdom."

- Benjamin Williams

"Honor is an absolute treasure of a book! Each and every chapter is engrossing and well written — and the lessons Janice teaches throughout are, as the title indicates, "Honor," to the reader. I was deeply touched by Janice Watts biblical insight, as well as, the wise counsel that she imparts in each lesson...I highly recommend it!"

– Jasmine Elaine

"Janice Watts Honor is an inspirational and rewarding guide to biblical principles of Honor. This clever hands-on approach gives readers steps and tools that enable them to understand how dishonor can plague your life. Through relatable experiences, scriptures, thought-provoking questions, and stirring points, Janice welcomes her audience to the joy of finding Honor in everything and brings awareness to the simple ways we can continually keep Honor. It is refreshing and reassuring to know that we can still have a life complete with love through honor, regardless of life's interruptions."

– Jokia Williams

HONOR

The Signet Of The Prophetic Voice

By: Janice Watts
Firebrand Publishing
Atlanta, Georgia USA

Copyright © 2017 by Janice Watts

All rights reserved. No part of this publication may be reproduced, distributed, or transmitted in any form or by any means, including photocopying, recording, or other electronic or mechanical methods, without the prior written permission of the publisher, except in the case of brief quotations embodied in critical reviews and certain other noncommercial uses permitted by copyright law. For permission requests, write to the publisher, addressed "Attention: Permissions Coordinator," at the address below.

Firebrand Publishing
2870 Peachtree Road Atlanta, Georgia 30305
https://firebrandpublishing.com
Ordering Information:
Quantity sales. Special discounts are available on quantity purchases by corporations, associations, and others. For details, contact the publisher at the address above.

THE HOLY BIBLE, NEW INTERNATIONAL VERSION®, NIV®

Copyright © 1973, 1978, 1984, 2011 by Biblica, Inc. TM

Used by permission. All rights reserved worldwide.

Printed in the United States of America
Publisher's Cataloging-in-Publication data
Watts, Janice.
Honor: The Signet Of The Prophetic Voice
p. cm.
ISBN 978-1-941907-06-1 paperback
ISBN 978-1-941907-07-8 eBook

First Edition
14 13 12 11 10 / 10 9 8 7 6 5 4 3 2 1

DEDICATION

I dedicate this book, first to the one whom my soul loveth, Abba. Without him, nothing by any means is possible. Secondly, I would like to honor my beautiful family. Jermar who has loved me beyond my faults, A'Necia who gave me hope when I was at a dead end, and Josiah, the son who God promised me. You are my prophetic promise, and mommy loves you. I am forever grateful for the people who have loved me, and pushed me, whether through persecution or through words of encouragement, I thank you. You are loved.

TABLE OF CONTENTS

Prophets of Honor 9

Hometown Challenges 14

Prophets Restore Honor 20

Dishonoring Vision 24

Honoring Vision 29

Honor is kingdom currency 33

Honor Increases your Oil 37

The Blessings of Honor 41

Repercussions of Dishonor: 44

Dishonor Denies Access 48

Honor Transcends Age 53

Obedience equates Honor 56

Teach Me to Rule 61

Acts of Dishonor & Consequences 65

Acts of Honor & Rewards 66

Scriptures on Honor 67

Scripture on Dishonor 70

Integrity 72

INTRODUCTION

THE LESSONS I'VE LEARNED early on in life, of loving the unlovable, have molded how I view people today. I often joke, that the Lord has allowed me to taste almost all that life offers, so that I can shower his people with love and affection, and relate to them on every level. As a young girl, I was overtaken by so much inner turmoil that the only way of outwardly expressing what I felt, was by living recklessly. I became dishonorable to my mother, dishonorable to my body, and most importantly, dishonorable to a God I'd only heard about, but had no relationship with. Growing up, as a young girl, I remember never feeling loved enough, although my dad would always shower me with "I love you's". There was a major void in me that searched for identity and love. It almost seemed as if the people I needed love from the most, were too busy to love me. The enemy used the void in my life to sow a root of rebellion and dishonor in my heart, that caused me to have no regard for myself or my family. It was as if I was surrounded by people, but no one could really hear me screaming on the inside.

JANICE WATTS

I recall experiencing so much hurt, as I watched my family and friend's moms' die in the streets during the crack epidemic. I soon began to have personal, and secret anxiety about life and death. This anxiety and fear that I couldn't release to anyone, caused me to become trapped in my own mind. These fears and anxiety, also allowed access to many demonic portals in my life.

By the time I was eight, I'd had so many sexual encounters, that I made them my little secrets. Being molested by a woman, to being molested and touched by grown men and boys, eventually became a normal part of my life. I completely had no self-worth, value, or honor for myself or anyone else, for that matter. Before I knew it, the inner enemy that I felt, was beyond what I could control. I remember being so disrespectful to my mother, that all she could say was, for me to "honor thy mother and father".

She would always remind me that my days would be short if I didn't stop, but somewhere somehow, I still couldn't get a grip on honoring my mother, because I didn't understand honor. Looking back, I think she did her best as a mom, but she worked so much and such long hours, that the relationship I desired to have with her, was nonexistent. It seemed to me, that the only communication we had was discipline and arguments. The lack of honor I had for myself, and for her or even for those that tried to love me, became over shadowed by my feelings of anxiety.

On my journey to salvation, the Lord allowed me to watch, as he began to bestow honor to my life, and also began to, publicly expose the enemy on my behalf. I never knew this side of the Lord. It was then, that my life began to have meaning!

I began to find my worth and value, as I watched God move on my behalf, without my interference. Through the years I've encountered heartbreak, sickness, poverty, depression, and grief. Although I stumbled and fell many times, the Lord has allowed me to recover.

In this place of restoration I've watched God pour honor on my life, when others counted me out. There's a message I hold dearly that I remind myself of at my most challenging times,

"Pick up your Crown."

This message has changed my life. It is as if Apostle Claudette was expecting me that day. God allowed that moment to replace my crown of Glory and Honor. The life of dishonor that I'd lead, a life of sexual perversions, and adultery, have been broken off of my life.

Now the glorious mantle of honor has been placed upon me. He gave me beauty for ashes, and restored to me the years that the enemy thought he took. He anointed my head with oil and my cup is running over, surely goodness and mercy shall follow me all the days of my life, because I will allow honor to have a continual voice in my life.

Our generation is in need of the voice of honor, because without it, we will continue the cycles of rebellion and disregard for one another.

HONOR

THIS BOOK INVITES YOU to give honor a voice in your life. When the voice of honor comes into your life the seasons of defensiveness will cease, because the King of glory will rise in your honor, and you will rise in his power.

We live in a time where barbaric and Babylonian characters have infiltrated the ranks of those who would call themselves, prophetic. With such an increase of prophetic individuals, we are seeing a decrease in prophetic accountability and honor. Many prophets today are finding themselves submitting to the seduction of rejection, which prompts their hearts to spew out dishonor upon individuals and ministries, that they have been assigned to catapult and til.

In over 10 years of serving in the ministry, I have discovered that honor is one of the keys to success in God, because it is a prominent principal of the Kingdom of God. Therefore, honor is essential in every area of life, including your family, ministry, and market place platforms. The absence of honor leaves us vulnerable to the spirit of shame and pride, therefore making you appear disreputable.

During my years of ministry, I have witnessed church divisions on different levels. Leaders of the flock can be responsible for massive divisions, and the creation of small exclusive groups, that divide the church. When we fail to honor one another, it is equal to failing to love.

It's been said that you can't disrespect the office and the individual, but I believe when we align ourselves to only respect the office, and not the person, we do ourselves and the individual a great disservice. We must maintain the heart that every joint supplies.

"From whom the whole body fitly joined together and compacted by that which every joint supplieth, according to the effectual working in the measure of every part, maketh increase of the body unto the edifying of itself in love "(Ephesians 4:16).

To only love the office of a postion is truly an issue within itself. While working with some can be difficult, we have been called to peace with all men.

"If it be possible, as much as lieth in you, live peaceably with all men" (Romans 12:18).

There is never an excuse for dishonor. Justice against injustice absolutely, but to dishonor simply because we've taken offense or have become irritated, is wrong. Being a person of honor must be an intentional action that is connected to your DNA.

"Be devoted to one another in love. Honor one another above yourselves" (Romans 12:10).

This is the time to restore honor to the prophetic office, and its correct and proper operation. We can start by recognizing what dishonor looks like, and applying key principles that will put us on track, and remove the blemishes of dishonor.

This book will give insight on how to allow the covenant of honor into your ministry, and also, give instructions on how to repair the breaches created through dishonor. We must infuse honor back into our Kingdom culture, conversations, and dynamics.

JANICE WATTS

PROPHETS OF HONOR

"WHEREFORE THE LORD GOD of Israel saith, I said indeed that thy house, and the house of thy father, should walk before me for ever: but now the LORD saith, Be it far from me; for them that honour me I will honour, and they that despise me shall be lightly esteemed" (1 Samuel 2:30).

The Lord is raising up prophetic voices. This includes every kingdom minded believer, that names the name of Christ, to restore honor back into the body of Christ. Our nation is making a desperate cry for dignity and honor to be restored. If we are to experience such changes, they must begin first in the Ecclesial, so that our nation can be permeated.

"If my people, which are called by my name, shall humble themselves, and pray, and seek my face, and turn from their wicked ways; then will I hear from heaven, and will forgive their sin, and will heal their land. Now look closely at this scripture not only is this a call to repentance for a nation but this is an unction to be humble and to denounce the heart of dishonor and disregard. Seek my face implies that the people had turn from the face of the Lord and in doing so dishonor is sown whenever we turn our face against the Lord" (2 Chronicles 7:14).

Our generation is, in need of authenticity, transparency, and integrity from the leaders of this generation. No longer will "do what I say and not what I do" concepts be tolerated. It's our time as a body to display this in action, and in deeds. We must interrupt the world system norms, with kingdom initiatives, principals, and agendas.

If we look closely at the types, patterns, and shadow, of what we see today in our society, we see a shadow of the times of Eli in the Ecclesial. We are witnessing, dishonor, disgrace, and a lack of integrity amongst the body of Christ.

HONOR

The sound of dishonor has been echoing loud, hence creating a pathway for deception and scandal to operate in the Ecclesial.

Because of the times ahead we are witnessing a rising in Hanna birth prophets with Samuel mandates rising to the forefronts.

Now, what is a Hanna birth prophet? I coined this phrase for prophets that have been birthed out of places that appeared barren, and thrust through the gates of intercessions. Prophets of this caliber have been conditioned in the priestly, established in honor, and will restore honor; as well as confront dishonors very existence.

We will find that many of the voices that the Lord is raising up in this hour, have suffered heavy blows of dishonor, shame, rejection and disregard. These vessels have been tried, tested, and found honorable in the sight of the Lord.

These voices have been face to face with their soul and chose not to cut their garments.

God is now placing the oil of honor in their hands, and on their mantles. These are vessels that don't look like the norm, don't sound like the norm, but they that have been appointed by God, to turn the world upside down. (Acts 17:6)

"Prophets of honor have been trained in kingdom etiquette and customs, by the king himself. The honor they carry goes beyond senior leadership, social status, and politics. (and is spread abroad unto the least of those).what do you mean? Prophets of this caliber will openly see your sin and restore you in private. One look at your displaced crown, and a prophet of honor instantly feels the heart of God, to insure that you are reinstated in glory and honor by placing your crown back in position" (Psalms 8:5).

Prophets of honor weep over sin and don't rejoice in iniquity. (1 Cor. 13:6)

You find that prophets that walk-in honor have a strong heart of intercession. Honorable prophets release intercession that is birthed out of love and compassion for the state of mankind.

We have witnessed an epidemic of so called prophetic voices that have risen in glory but, have allowed their mantle to be purchased, bought and sold, and therefore have lost sight of purpose, promise and destiny.

Typically, these individuals lack integrity and honor by depreciating Gods creation to the cost of a dollar bill, or a platform, of status. We as the body of believers, represent the prophetic voice of the Lord in the earth, and we must pursue the heart of the Lord to align our character.

How we represent Christ is extremely important for the people of God, because it speaks to the reliability of the source from which we speak, whom we serve and who we declare sent us. We should be ever so sensitive in knowing that God will not be mocked by any of our misleading intentions or facades. Prophets, as well as all believers, must be intentional about aligning our hearts with the heart of God.

So many cultures throughout our world teach honor as a custom, and still we find that honor is absent in our society. Our lack of honor has displaced our integrity and overshadowed our voice in today's society.

Kingdom attributes are extremely important as ambassadors of the kingdom of God, because these attributes speak to validity. So, now we must go back to the basics and begin to teach the customs of the kingdom of God, by accurately disciplining the body of believers, and exemplifying his nature to a lost world. We must refuse to raise up replicas of our own names or brands and raise up the son of God. We must do this, not only in name, but also embody his nature.

HOMETOWN CHALLENGES

"AND HE WENT OUT from thence, and came into his own country; and his disciples follow him.

And when the sabbath day was come, he began to teach in the synagogue: and many hearing him were astonished, saying, From whence hath this man these things? and what wisdom is this which is given unto him, that even such mighty works are wrought by his hands? not this the carpenter, the son of Mary, the brother of James, and Joses, and of Juda, and Simon?

HONOR

and are not his sisters here with us? And they were offended at him.

But Jesus said unto them, A prophet is not without honor, but in his own country, and among his own kin, and in his own house.

And he could there do no mighty work, save that he laid his hands upon a few sick folk, and healed them.

And he marveled because of their unbelief. And he went round about the villages, teaching" (Mark 6:1-6).

One of the many challenges that many prophets face is confrontation with hometown spirits. When contending in your familiar space, quite often, one of the many hindrances is those that are familiar with you personally.

Some may be familiar with your gift, and sometimes even your past. When challenged by hometown resistance you come face to face with dishonor, rejection and contention.

This can be a critical time for most prophets because what is familiar to you has the ability to affect your emotional and mental state. You must be cautious in pushing past the rejection of those you know and love, so that you may carry out the assignment for those that are pulling on your mantle.

Dishonor and rejection are sent to oppress you, thus sabotaging your season of emergence. However, the truth is there, a remnant that needs what God has placed in your life and on your life.

We must keep in mind that no matter the climate, we are called by God for the sake of his people and the kingdom for such a time as this. (Esther 4:14)

In recent years, we have seen the results produced by many prophets, responding to the lack of honor with retaliation, by projecting dishonor to those that they feel have slighted them, or cheated them out of honor.

We make a grave error when we the people of God strike out to command or demand honor. As prophets, your very roots are restoration and releasing the fathers heart to his people. Dishonor disrupts, as well as challenges your authenticity, integrity, and reputation. We can't allow the vile effects of dishonor to stop us from doing what we have been assigned to do.

Receiving honor from the people as a prophet is not your responsibility. It is the responsibility, and choice of the people of God to honor the prophetic office.

HONOR

We must be concisely aware that honor most be bestowed on every part of the body of Christ, and not just limited to the prophets. Many prophets try to force, manipulate and demand honor. This shouldn't be so.

"He that receiveth a prophet in the name of a prophet shall receive a prophet's reward; and he that receiveth a righteous man in the name of a righteous man shall receive a righteous man's reward" (Mathew 10:4).

If God has so ordained and endorsed an individual, their responsibility is to the people. Your assignment is to hear clearly, see accurately, and release the heart of God no matter what is being perpetuated, unless instructed otherwise. We are not to fight for our honor, but to contend for the honor of the King and his kingdom, the faith. (Jude 1:3)

For so many prophets the scope of familiarity can serve to cause issues when respect becomes a factor. Our greatest rejection is more likely bought on by those whom we love and hold dear to our hearts. Rejection is a symptom of dishonor that masks itself in many other manifestations such as shame, hatred, jealousy, envy, backbiting and bitterness.

Prophetic people, if not in a state of stability, can be overcome by the spirit of rejection, and force themselves into a mental cave.

As a prophetic voice, when you bring honor to the forefront of your ministry and office, you will begin to master the spirit of rejection, loneliness, and fear.

When there is honor on your mantle, where once you were rejected, you will now become sought after.

Honor changes your name, and enhances your reputation. Dishonor mars your name, confuses your identity, while disrupting the assignment, and hindering your destiny.

"And they shall call them, The holy people, The redeemed of the LORD: and thou shalt be called, Sought out, A city not forsaken" (Isaiah. 62: 12).

HONOR
PRAYER

Dear Lord, we come to you in recognition that you are a most holy God. We further recognize that you are seeking a holy people, and we ask that you step into our space, and restore every place that we have sown dishonor, discord, and dissension amongst the brethren. Lord, come in and remove the cloak of shame bought on by dishonor.

Revive. Restore, and renew our hearts again with yours, that we may walk as one loving people, and encourage one another, just as you have called us to.

Cleanse our hands of any innocent blood that we have shed, and equip us with honor to repair the breaches.

Purge our hearts of corruption and spiritual perjury, that has caused us to falsely accuse and dishonor our brethren.

So, Lord we say thank you for deliverance, thank you for restoration of honor upon our lives this day. In Jesus name.

PROPHETS RESTORE HONOR

PROPHETS RESTORE HONOR. Our world is in desperate need of honor. The principles of honor have been completely defaced in our churches and society.

Human life is so devalued in today's world, that murder is the norm in most major communities, racism has become mainstream once again, and fights have become pleasurable entertainment.

Our inability to see the value in one another, has placed our country in moral crisis. Our behavior resulted in commandments, morals, and biblical principles being shunned by the world, and weakly enforced by the church.

All of which has completely shattered and distorted the moral compass of our nation, and has lead us into a downward spiral.

We need honorable voices in this hour, to arise and reveal the value of life, through the power of the resurrected Christ to a lost world.

Why has honor, integrity and reverence become so distant to the world? They have become faint in the body of Christ. Many in the Body have lived high on prestige, preference and politics for decades, while they're seated in authority, and ignore, underserved populations of people.

This behavior is a complete disgrace to the Lord, because it completely defies kingdom principals, standards and order. There has been a trend, where prophetic voices have reduced their gift, down to the size of a hundred-dollar bill, while still leaving a body of people in shambles, with no direction.

For some, this behavior has become so normal, it exemplifies the diminishing honor that many have for the Lord.

"For the name of God is blasphemed among the Gentiles through you, as it is written" (Romans 2:24).

When we commit such acts, we create space for hearts to be turned against God.

We, as prophets, must shun taking on celebrity status, and becoming untouchable to the people of God. When we become untouchable to the people, we now become unavailable to God.

As Prophets we should always deal in honor. Our assignment is to restore honor, where shame has ruled, and bring the hearts of the people back in alignment with the father's heart.

Once the cloak of shame is removed, so also will be the scales that blur our spiritual awareness and sensitivity. Honor is the resolve to the moral death in our society. It releases the kings provision and protection into our midst, by reinstating kingdom alignment and positioning.

Every prophet and kingdom minded believer should walk heavy in honor, whether it is reciprocated or not. Honor is the very nature of Christ.

If we are to name the name of Christ, we are to walk in honor, love and integrity. Many leaders have been seeking out solutions to deal with the sins of stagnation, bitterness, backbiting, and confusion, that have been running through the their local assemblies.

Truthfully, it must be recognized that because of the lack of reverence for God, it's easy to dishonor those that we are assigned to walk in close proximity with.

HONOR

We as prophets, have to recognize that dishonor is the doorway to sin. We need repentance to bring us back into righteous standing with Jesus, by restoring our relationship with him.

Honor is one of the keys to shutting down demonic entry, by barring access to discord, dissension, and division. I believe this speaks to the principle of guarding your heart with all diligence. (Prov. 4:23)

We are unable to guard our heart if the word of God is not hide there. (Psalms 119:11)

Honor reveals the heart of man by shining light on the value we place on our relationship with Abba as well as our love for one another. To restore honor, we must restore love. We must have love that burns for God and that will cover his people. Honor is simply an extension of his love, we are commanded to love one another.

"Above all, keep fervent in your love for one another, because love covers a multitude of sins" (1 Peter 4:8 NASB).

"A new commandment I give unto you, That ye love one another; as I have loved you, that ye also love one another. By this shall all men know that ye are my disciples, if ye have love one to another" (John 13:34-35 KJV).

DISHONORING VISION

IT IS OF GREAT IMPORTANCE as prophets, that we honor vision. Without honoring the vision of our assigned place, we open the doors to frustration and become unproductive.

This results in an open invitation to a vagabond or renegade spirit. Our assignment isn't to go in and change the vision of a house, our assignment is to bring clarity and foresight to what the Lord is saying, concerning the direction of his people.

When we don't allow room for the leading of the holy spirit, we may tend to operate with a spirit of deception, control, and manipulation, to create what we see versus what the Lord is saying.

This is Jezebel at her finest when we give her access. We should remember even if we see instances and circumstances that may not be properly aligned, we need to be sure to get clarity and strategic plans from the Lord.

This will avoid going on a tangent or war path to verbally demolish or criticize the set man or woman, that our Lord has set in place. When we do entertain such negative behaviors, we will produce unproductive criticism of the leader and the vision, therefore becoming a hindrance to the work.

If we allow ourselves to become a hindrance to the plans of God, we put ourselves in the path of hard rebuke. (Mark 8:33)

We find that Peter, attempted to interfere with the will of God and was instantly rebuked, so we must be mindful of our response. Behavior of this nature can become extremely dangerous for prophets, conflicting with our assignment to edify, exhort and comfort, while also being able to build, plant, pull down, root out, destroy and so forth. If your prophetic mantle only stirs you to destroy, it's time to revisit the altar.

We are to flow, according to Gods divine layout. We prophets, operate as eyes, ears, and voices for the ministry,

God has assigned us to. When we allow our opinion to override the voice of God, we can steer the people of God in the wrong direction. This will create a mess instead of a message.

When a trusted prophet or prophetic voice in a ministry is hard pressed against vision they cause dissension, discord and division amongst the brethren. (Romans 16: 17-18)

I have personally witnessed a prophet of great status and caliber that raises up in dishonor, concerning the vision of the house. They have the potential and capability to sabotage the work, and raising up an insurrection in the ministry. How is this even possible one might ask?

It's simple., They believe and trust the prophet, as they should. However, the moment the prophet raises up against the vision those that aren't rooted and grounded will easily be dislodged outside of the timing of God.

When this happens, the prophet has just sown seeds, that will spring forward into an unnecessary revolt. So now, those that should be in support of their leader's vision, are now dishonoring their headship because of your level of influence in the ministry. This leads to opening portals in your own life and ministry.

"And Miriam and Aaron spake against Moses because of the Ethiopian woman whom he had

**married: for he had married an Ethiopian woman "
(Numbers 12:1).**

"And they said, Hath the LORD indeed spoken only by Moses? hath he not spoken also by us? And the LORD heard it" (Numbers 12:2).

We notice that Miriam dishonored Moses in the sight of God and the people. Her sin hindered the mobility of the entire camp; so not only was she affected but those around her were as well.

Moses had to stand in a place of prayer so that Miriam wouldn't die in the place of dishonor. Clearly, we see that dishonor is not a light offense in the sight of the Lord. We also see an entire movement was hindered, because dishonor had a voice and a vision.

It's important that we don't attempt to cast vision where the Lord has already set vision in place. God will hold us spiritually accountable for the way we lead and guide his people.

Many prophets are looking for ministries where they can enlarge their following while, neglecting the assignment to undergird and strengthen the people of God. When we sow into another's vision we can wait in expectation for the Lord to place the same honor on us.

"And if ye have not been faithful in that which is another man's, who shall give you that which is your own?" (Luk 16:12).

HONORING VISION

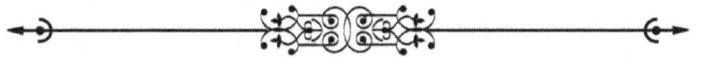

How do we attain insight or come into agreement with the vision of the house?

Prayer is fundamental, when seeking insight into being a blessing to the ministry, God has aligned you with.

What if I don't agree with the vision of the house?

If, you don't agree with the vision of the house, and the Lord has set you in this ministry, your next question should be,

"Lord what is my assignment here?"

We must remember its acceptable to ask questions.

All of these aspects are so important when dealing with vision, because we want to arrive to the appointed destination on time. If we don't know the vision or support the vision, we are more than likely going to wander in circles, because we lack honor for the vision, mandate and the leaders.

When we recognize the vision, and align it with the assignment, it makes running easy. (habbakuh 2:2)

Too often we connect to the assignment without pure motives, therefore causing drama and derailment in the lives of others.

"And the LORD answered me, and said, Write the vision, and make it plain upon tables, that he may run that readeth it" (habbakuh 2:2).

"For the vision is yet for an appointed time, but at the end it shall speak, and not lie: though it tarry, wait for it; because it will surely come, it will not tarry" (habbakuh 2:3).

What happens when honor is cast on a vision? When prophets honor vision, destiny and Kyros is aligned.

As prophets, our responsibility is discerning the climate and timing of God. The moment we align and honor vision, ministries begin to thrust forward, just from your submitted prayer, presence and support of what God is doing.

The prophetic mantle carries many characteristics such as creativity, wealth, direction, healing, deliverance and many more. All these aspects are needed when vision is being pushed forward and carried out by the body.

Sight is extremely important in vision, because it makes building easy without having to grope in dark places.

Many ministries are dealing with the groping concept, because they have yet to come in line with the prophetic voice of God. The prophetic is the sober voice of God, that removes the spiritual blur from our eyes, takes the confusion out of the mind, and tames our speech, while aligning our direction.

Sobriety is vital for citizens of the kingdom. Absent a sober spirit, we are exposed and open to spiritual demonic entanglement.

"They grope in the dark without light, and he maketh them to stagger like a drunken man" (Job 12:25).

Without prophetic actuation, you can build, but maintenance becomes hard, and ministry becomes stale. Prophets have an assignment to recognize when it's time for refreshing and to call forth the water needed, when drought or stagnation appears.

Without the prophetic presence, ministries become comfortable with hearing their own voices and responding to their own heartbeat. The prophetic maintains the fire behind a God given vision, and echoes the fathers heart throughout the process.

HONOR IS KINGDOM CURRENCY

"**FOR THIS CAUSE PAY YE tribute also: for they are God's ministers, attending continually upon this very thing. Render therefore to all their dues: tribute to whom tribute is due; custom to whom custom; fear to whom fear; honor to whom honour**" (Romans 13:6-8).

Just as currency is exchanged in the natural world, currency is also exchanged in the kingdom of God, through the system and principle of honor.

Many have tried to spend what they have not earned, and earn when they have not given. Just as we need currency to purchase necessities for daily living, we need honor as spiritual currency.

When we operate without honor we become spiritually dry, stale, and unproductive. When we become spiritually disposed, all of our resources become tied up, dried up, and we now need the representation of mercy, brought on by true repentance to release our assets, therefore redeeming the time. Dishonor places a hold on your account that, can't be afforded in your life.

Many take light of sowing in honor, for one it's not taught and secondly, we are in a time where everyone is demanding some form of honor on so many levels.

It is well for us to honor all. It's also well, that we would store up honor, in our store houses, by sowing in love. Storing up honor isn't simply remembering all the good others have done for you, it's about embracing and remembering the love of God and the honor he has placed upon you.

Storing up honor is a reminder that we all have sinned and fallen short of his glory. We should not use this as an occasion to sin, but as a route to extend mercy to those around us.

HONOR

According to scripture we have been crowned with glory and honor,

"For thou hast made him a little lower than the angels, and hast crowned him with glory and honour" (Psalms 8:5).

Being crowned speaks of our completion in Christ as joint heirs in his kingdom. (Romans 8:17)

Our very nature in the kingdom should be one of honor. The sooner we recognize the truth in who we are, the sooner we will place things in the kingdom back, into proper perspective.

Honor is one of the highest levels of exchange in the kingdom. It speaks to the value of God's creation. For so long we've devalued God and we've devalued creation.

The spirit of the Lord is summoning us to repentance, and to a place of restored honor. Without the currency of honor, our level of influence will digress, or become null and void. Whenever influence is dismantled many begin to operate in a payola system.

What is payola you ask?

It's pay to play.

For so many seasons many have been buying their way in the kingdom of God. Some have bought their way onto the pulpit, or the media, or to the market place, and into the hearts of the people.

However, that season has come to a halt, and the remnant that God is raising up will carry such a mantle of honor, that carnal means won't be necessary.

The favor of God will provide resources and unstoppable wells.

HONOR INCREASES YOUR OIL

HONOR WILL INCREASE YOUR LIFE, just look at Mary Magdalene. Don't just look at her in a carnal systematic way of thinking, look at the spiritual connotation of what happened in her encounter with Jesus.

When Mary Magdalene broke her alabaster box of oil on Jesus, she poured out of her substance what was precious and costly, on the one worthy of honor.

She placed her worship on the honorable one.

Wow! What a statement of love, that her brokenness was exemplified in this natural but, yet divine experience.

Mary's, act of worship was such a powerful depiction of honor. She was a woman that had been cloaked in shame and robed in disgrace, but she came with what she had, and cast honor where it would be received and requite.

Many who observed her act questioned it, and criticized it, but, she didn't allow that to stop her worship. Jesus honored her so much so that while the religious where untouchable, he became touchable to a woman once shunned by society.

When we look at this narrative we see Mary received an increase for her act of obedience, and experienced a divine encounter. Her act of worship and adoration, still speaks for her today.

The honored she poured out became a memorial. When we pour out our substance unto the Lord he will respond to the pure in heart,

Matthew 5:8 says:

"...blessed are the pure in heart for they shall see God."

This shows us that whenever we leave the presence of the Lord feeling empty handed, it's because we never poured anything out, or the condition of our hearts was not conducive for the encounter.

This also applies, when we expect to receive impartation from the lives of those assigned to groom us and catapult us forward. You can't dishonor the source and expect a divine impartation or release.

When you sow in dishonor you will surely reap the same harvest. Often when we are stuck in a spiritual cycle, we have pulled on the oil dishonorably or have sown in dishonor.

The Lord has positioned people in our lives to help with the production and birthing process, but we also must not reject the tillers that God has placed in our lives.

When we dismiss those that we are to honor we dismiss the miraculous. Mary Magdalene recognized the one who could place honor in her life, and she went for it, and in return it was counted unto her as a historical act of worship.

Honor will cause you to experience the divine presence, and encounter glory.

There's so much to learn from Mary's encounter with the Lord. Her reverence for God gave her access to his manifested glory, and has been placed down as memorial throughout the ages.

"Verily I say unto you, Wheresoever this gospel shall be preached throughout the whole world, this also that she hath done shall be spoken of for a memorial of her" (Mark 14:9).

JANICE WATTS

One small act in the eyes of many, has become a platform for generations. When we expand the way we have bottled up Kingdom principles, we will leave legacies of oil for generations to come. The honor you sow now will still speak for you when you are gone.

THE BLESSINGS OF HONOR

SO NOW LET'S have a look at how fruitful honor can affect your life.

Now we should be careful not to sow a false sense of honor, to receive a crop that we haven't really earned.

It doesn't work.

Just like everything else in the kingdom, the Lord sees and knows our heart. A false honor system won't release an honorable crop, but once we tap into the place of honor blessings are released.

- Honor releases dominion
- Honor inspires unity
- Honor Increases favor

- Honor gives you access
- Honor removes the cloak of shame
- Honor restores reputation
- Honor attracts Kings
- Honor attaches you to Glory
- Honor covers you in love
- Honor aligns kyros
- Honor transcends Generation
- Honor speaks for you
- Honor changes your DNA
- Honor Silences your enemies
- Honor increases your prophetic influence
- Honor will finance your vision
- Honor shuts the mouth of the Grave

When you tap into the importance of having honor on your mantle it will make the calling on your life much easier. Where you've struggled before with people and assignments, things will get easier, enabling you to operate in a sweat less anointing.

HONOR
PRAYER:

Father, as I begin to walk this new Journey of Honor, I thank you for the blessings that flow from honor, that are being restored into my life. I thank you for the new wells that are opening for me. I declare Rehoboth in the atmosphere, for you have made room for me. I pray for continual awareness and sensitivity to your presence, and your heart. As I go forward in the things that concern your kingdom, enhance my ability to operate in kingdom customs, and pour out the blessings of double honor on my life, that not only will I be a giver of honor but a recipient of honor as well. Thank you for increasing my knowledge and accountability in the spirit of honor, in Jesus Name I pray, Amen.

REPERCUSSIONS OF DISHONOR

LET'S LOOK AT the backlash manufactured by dishonor.

We talked earlier, about how our culture and most of our society norms are embedded in dishonor and devaluing one another. We see this in the mass racial divides, cultural divides, and economic divides.

If we would open our eyes beyond our small scope of influence, we would see that the church is even playing Russian roulette in some of these games.

The church is also serving as enforcer to a lot of the uproar. Sunday service is one of the most segregated times in our country. We've reduced worship activities to pigment and melanin.

We've determined who can play our game of politics, based on their financial status and we've reduced individuals to cultural stereotypes. In all this we have failed in love and honor and have allowed the fallen state of man to speak louder than the redemption power of the kingdom.

If we can't honor one another here on earth, we can't possibly think we will gain access into the kingdom of God. Our inability to love and honor one another speaks volumes, to our heart for the father.

Dishonor is accompanied by many harsh realities. Dishonor is iniquity of the flesh, brought on by the fallen nature of mankind. A Dishonor is promoted by the enemy himself, the father of lies and ring leader of dishonor.

Let's take a brief look:

- Dishonor brings death
- Dishonor sows discord
- Dishonor uncovers and exposes
- Dishonor abhors bitterness
- Dishonor sabotages
- Dishonor seeks to destroy

- Dishonor breaks covenant
- Dishonor pulls you in captivity
- Dishonor sheds innocent blood
- Dishonor breaks rank
- Dishonor brings insubordination
- Dishonor will abort the birthing process
- Dishonor will force you into slavery
- Dishonor will cause you to be bought
- Dishonor will steal your identity
- Dishonor brings competitiveness
- Dishonor will produce a vagabond spirit
- Dishonor will interrupt the building process
- Dishonor undermines authority
- Dishonor stifles spiritual growth
- Dishonor produces cults instead of kingdom
- Dishonor will cause spiritual/natural adultery
- Dishonor can manifest through spiritual incest

This list could be so much longer. I'm sure individually, we can think of things that have manifested in our lives based on dishonor we've perpetuated.

HONOR

So, it's imperative that we began to examine our lives, relationships, and the way we conduct ourselves by reexamining the code of honor in our lives.

DISHONOR DENIES ACCESS

SO MANY HAVE FOUND themselves walking in the potholes and cycles that the spirit of dishonor carries into our lives. When we embrace the language and mindset of dishonor, we create a system for our lives, ministry, and family included.

Dishonor denies you access to the promises God intended for you to have. If we take a brief look based off Hams actions in exposing Noah, (Gen. 9:18-29) we see that disgrace shifted his level of operation, access, and position. Ham's role and influence changed, just from one act of dishonor.

Dishonor brings premature death as it interrupts the flourishing power of life that is bought forward by honoring the Lord with your substance.

We often only think of substance as material things, but we are substance, and the fruit that we produce from walking in the word of God is also substance.

To disregard the word of God brings dishonor and death, and denies us access to favor, longevity, and increase.

Dishonor denies you access by causing you to be stagnated in a spiritual wilderness or dry place. What should have been a three day journey now becomes forty years, and eventually the death of your aspirations, to reach the promises of God.

In other words we find ourselves attempting to ascend to the presence of the Lord with unclean hands and a crowded and confused heart.

"Who shall ascend onto the hill of the LORD? Who shall stand in his holy place? He that hath clean hands, and a pure heart; who hath not lifted up his soul unto vanity, nor sworn deceitfully. He shall receive the blessing from the LORD, and righteousness from the God of his salvation" (Psalms 24:3-5).

Dishonor, is an issue of the heart that sets out to demolish and destroy our alignments, alliances and reputation. The reality is that dishonor denies you access to destiny, making you become hindered, and making established destinations delayed or unreachable.

Dishonor causes open doors that have been established for your mantle, to close in your face, and slowly progress, to spoil your harvest.

HONOR
DECLARATION:

I declare that dishonor will no longer hinder my mobility, or delay my arrival to my destination.

I declare that the seeds that have been brought forth with dishonor are now being pulled from the root, by the love of God.

I declare that honor will be poured out on my family, my mantle, and my ministry.

I declare that when people see me that they will see honor

I declare that every snare and trap that dishonor sets up for me is abolished, removed, destroyed and displaced.

I declare that my reputation in all places secular and kingdom be restored

I declare favor shall follow me, because I honor God and his people.

I declare that I walk in Kingdom Customs, with the kingdom's agenda and a kingdom mindset.

I declare that God has aligning me with honorable alignments and disconnected every dishonorable connection.

I declare that I have been trained to dine with kings, and I shall have my seat at the table

I declare that disgrace, shame, fear, and hidden agenda are removed from my heart.

I declare that I shall be named by a new name.

I declare I am sought out, not forsaken, or bought with a price, crowned with glory and honor and set in a large place.

I declare that because I walk in honor that I shall be clothed with the blessing of Jabez, that I would be blessed indeed, and my territory would be enlarged.

I declare that every declaration is sealed with the blood of the Lamb, and I shall have a great testimony.

In Jesus Name.

HONOR TRANSCENDS AGE

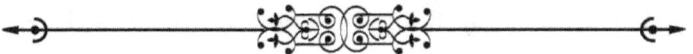

Honor is not an issue of age, and should not be withheld based on that fact. I felt it was extremely important to add this chapter on honor transcending age, because we miss this valuable nugget so often.

We forget and press on so often, striving to reach our destiny, and tend to leave our young people behind. This is a great disregard to our youth, and the heart of the father.

To dishonor individuals based on age, is a disservice to the Lord. When we dishonor, devalue, and disregard our children, we create a climate of rejection, disrespect, malice, and rebellion.

We see that when we breed dishonor to our children, they often grow up with a disregard for the Lord. This very widespread issue for parents in leadership, as well as parents that are overly active in the church, and detached from home. We must teach and exhibit honor in our homes, so that our children will walk in what they see. Lead by example, rather than leading vocally, only.

"And whoso shall receive one such little child in my name received me" (Matthew 18:5).

But whoso shall offend one of these little ones which believe in me, it were better for him that a millstone were hanged about his neck, and that he were drowned in the depth of the sea" (Matthew 18:6).

"Take heed that ye despise not one of these little ones; for I say unto you, That in heaven their angels do always behold the face of my Father which is in heaven" (Matthew 18:10).

In honoring our children, we must not forget to minister to their needs. Just as we discern, labor, prophecy, and prayer with adults, we must find the same passion for our children. They are the upcoming prophetic voices, and what will it say of us if we don't train them in the customs of the kingdom, by teaching them how to rule.

HONOR

We will have created a generation of superstars rather than prophets, priests and kings.

We can't expect the world to teach honor to our younger generation. That is up to us whether you have children or not. We are the standard.

OBEDIENCE EQUATES HONOR

"**...AND SAMUEL SAID, Hath the LORD as great delight in burnt offerings and sacrifices, as in obeying the voice of the LORD? Behold, to obey is better than sacrifice, and to hearken than the fat of rams.**

For rebellion is as the sin of witchcraft, and stubbornness is as iniquity and idolatry. Because thou hast rejected the word of the LORD, he hath also rejected thee from being king" (1 Samuel 15:22-23).

HONOR

Let's look at obedience as is relates to honor. When we look at Saul, we can learn so much about honor and dishonor. Saul was instructed by the prophet Samuel, according to the word of the Lord.

He was instructed to fight against Amalek and destroy everything concerning them. If we take a look at what Saul actually did versus what he was instructed to do, we will see that Saul operated in great disregard to the Lord and to the instruction of the prophet Samuel.

This is so critical, because we will see that Saul considered his sacrifice to be of more importance then his obedience. He not only disobeyed, but he also quickly blamed the people as well.

Today we see this exact same thing. Many believe because they have sacrificed time, money, and other resources that it holds more weight than their obedience, but truthfully, God is concerned about our character and integrity over our sacrifice.

When we disobey God, it equates to witch craft. (1Sam. 15:23)

Saul's disobedience spoke of his character, integrity and heart. Obedience, starts in the mind, and is displayed through the actions we carry out. This form of obedience is derived from the word shema, which means to hear. When we truly hear God, we will encompass the mental ability to obey.

In Saul's disobedience, he dishonored the Lord and was judged, according to his actions. Dishonor will dethrone you from a set place. We must be careful, that when God gives us specific insight and instruction, we must follow after the heart of God with all diligence.

As Leaders, we must not prefer the recognition of man over the voice of God. Whenever a leader finds themselves in this place of abhorring recognition, we began to seek personal honor over the honor of the Lord.

Saul asked Samuel to honor him before the people, even after knowing he had been stripped of his kingdom. Many today are operating with a stripped mantle, because they have chosen to be the people's choice, over Gods choice.

God is raising up a company of prophetic voices that will confront dishonor in the ranks, without intimidation. Prophets that have been released to deal with leaders have a strong heart to avenge the honor of the Lord and his people.

When we as leaders operate in disobedience we are held accountable to our actions. Saul lacked accountability and became an unreliable source by opening access to witch craft into his life.

HONOR

Whenever leaders plainly ignore the voice of the Lord and lead people astray, according to their personal hearts desires, they become active participants in witchcraft. Every leader must strive to serve honorably, and be honorable.

Disobedience to God will cause us to live comfortably amongst the very things, we have been instructed to kill. When we become willing partners with sin and corruption, we set in place the atmosphere that we are willing to accept.

The charge being placed on the prophets of this hour is to drive out, slay, and utterly destroy sin and corruption in the midst of his people. As prophets, we must be prophetic and priestly and willing to destroy what God hates, and love what he loves. In driving out sin, we must not destroy or injure the vessel, but deal with the spirits at work and in operation.

Honor breaks the back of compromise in the body of Christ. We must endeavor to walk in honor and establish the kingdom of God, and carry out his mandate. Priestly prophets are needed in this hour to establish order and honor.

We must not be moved. Whenever you encounter a spiritual Saul, you must stand firm on biblical principle and obedience to the voice of the Lord. Spiritual Saul's are secretly rebellious and dishonorable at heart. These types of leaders seek honor, all while being dishonorable to God.

It's amazing that most dishonorable leaders look for loyalty in the flock, while they themselves lack tremendously in loyalty and integrity. We can't allow our behavior to be in contradictory, over those that we are set to lead, while expecting to receive honor, while we are inadvertently sowing exactly what we don't plan to reap.

It's dishonorable, however, we can outwardly mask being honorable and prestigious, while secretly being covetous, jealous, and dishonorable.

Saul's only attempt to mask his hearts deception, was by requesting honor that he did not deserve, and only seeking forgiveness from Samuel. As prophets of honor, we must not fear or adhere to any perverse request from man, that disregard the will of God, concerning his people.

TEACH ME TO RULE

A KING WITHOUT HONOR becomes a tyrant or dictator.

We as believers in the kingdom of God have been set in place as rulers and leaders in our generation. The way we rule will determine how we build.

Whenever we take on tyrannical behavior as a ruler, we become cruel and oppressive to the people of God. This mimics a form of modern day slavery.

A ruler without honor will demand honor, while breaking the back of the people economically and socially. This type of behavior displays a modern day pharaoh spirit. We are seeing this in many assemblies where leaders are taking on the people of God, as their prized possessions, and demanding to be served.

Behavior of this nature is the opposite of the Kingdom mindset: that teaches, the greatest in the kingdom, are those that serve.

"But he that is greatest among you shall be your servant. And whosoever shall exalt himself shall be abased; and he that shall humble himself shall be exalted" (Matthew 23:11-12).

Whenever we as leaders operate in a tyrannical manner we dishonor God and become brutal task masters to the people of God.

Kings are trained in honor. All throughout history we see where the very act of dishonoring the king could cost you your life. We learn from the book of Esther that the idea of coming to the King un-summoned could cost you your life.

The honor that was on Esther's life, her favor and obedience gave her access to the king and his heart. When we move in the principal of honor, it will take us to a place where denial and delay must bow. Honor will cause your enemies to be handed over to you.

"All the king's servants, and the people of the king's provinces, do know, that whosoever, whether man or

woman, shall come unto the king into the inner court, who is not called, there is **one law of his to put** him **to death, except such to whom the king shall hold out the golden scepter, that he may live: but I have not been called to come in unto the king these thirty days" - (Esther 4:11).**

Then the king held out the golden scepter toward Esther. So Esther arose, and stood before the king, and said, "If it please the king, and if I have found favor in his sight, and the thing seem right before the king, and I be pleasing in his eyes, let it be written to reverse the letters devised by Haman the son of Hammedatha the Agagite, which he wrote to destroy the Jews which are in all the king's provinces: For how can I endure to see the evil that shall come unto my people? or how can I endure to see the destruction of my kindred?" Then the king Ahasuerus said unto Esther the queen, and to Mordecai the Jew, "Behold, I have given Esther the house of Haman, and him they have hanged upon the gallows, because he laid his hand upon the Jews" (Esther 8:4-7).

When we are honorable we render the accuser powerless over our destiny, and gain authority to abolish demonic plots, ploys, and schemes, spoken over your life and the lives of many people.

Enclosing, honor to many in our generation, has become an outdated principle with no validity, in our current day and age. This is far from true, the conditions in our world say otherwise.

Our lack of honor has increased demonic activity, therefore causing us complete torment and destruction on many levels around us. It is the assignment of the people of God to take responsibility for what we see.

Without ownership of our surroundings, ministries or families, we will continue forward in turmoil and confusion. When you as a prophet of God adopt a heart of honor, what flows out of you will be the fathers heart for his people.

Honor will change the way you view every aspect of the kingdom of God. No longer will we look at, and determine who should be saved based on preference or stature. We will focus more on building individuals, instead of man made structures.

Honor changes the way you see church and do church, it challenges your preference, thus pushing you to look inside the cup rather then focusing on the outside of the cup. Honor will change your view and enlarge your territory.

HONOR

ACTS OF DISHONOR & CONSEQUENCES

Names:	Scripture:	Consequence:
Adam, Eve	Genesis. 3:1-24	<ul><li>Banishment from the promise.</li><li>Death</li><li>Grounds Cursed</li></ul>
Moses	Numbers 20:8-12	<ul><li>Unable to possess the Land.</li><li>Died in the wilderness</li></ul>
Ham (Noah's Son)	Genesis 9:18, Genesis 10:32	Demoted spiritually and Naturally
David	2 Samuel 13-15	<ul><li>Ran out his kingdom</li><li>Daughter disgraced by son</li></ul>
Saul	1 Samuel 15	<ul><li>Kingdom taken from him.</li><li>Rejected as king</li></ul>
Judas	Matthew 27: 3-8, Acts 1:18-19	<ul><li>Betrays the Lord</li><li>Dies dishonorably</li></ul>

ACTS OF HONOR & REWARDS

Names:	Scripture:	Rewards:
Ruth	Ruth 1:14-16, Ruth 3:6-18, Ruth 4	Naomi was redeemed, she was able to glean freely in the field
Abraham	Gensis 12:1-3	The nation of the earth were blessed through his obedience
Solomon	1 kings 3	Blessed with wisdom and wealth
David	1 Samuel 24:3-7, 1 Samuel 24:8-15	Davids kingdom was blessed, and extended
Job	Job 42:7-10	Jobs life and resources were restored as well as the judgement against his friends removed
Shadrach, Meshach and Abednego	Daniel 3	A decree was made to honor God, they were promoted
Hanna	1 Samuel 1:10	Gave birth, produced, honored her word
Samuel	1 Samuel 3	Clear hearing, honored as prophet in Israel

SCRIPTURES ON HONOR

1Peter 2:17-18

Honor all men; love the brotherhood, fear God, honor the king. Servants, be submissive to your masters with all respect. . ."

2 Timothy 2:21 ESV

Therefore, if anyone cleanses himself from what is dishonorable, he will be a vessel for honorable use, set apart as holy, useful to the master of the house, ready for every good work.

Romans 12:10

Verse Concepts
Be devoted to one another in brotherly love; give preference to one another in honor;

1 Timothy 5:17

Verse Concepts
The elders who rule well are to be considered worthy of double honor, especially those who work hard at preaching and teaching.

1 Peter 2:17-19 ESV

Honor everyone. Love the brotherhood. Fear God. Honor the emperor. Servants, be subject to your masters with all respect, not only to the good and gentle but also to the unjust. For this is a gracious thing, when, mindful of God, one endures sorrows while suffering unjustly.

Ephesians 6:1-4 ESV

Children, obey your parents in the Lord, for this is right. "Honor your father and mother" (this is the first commandment with a promise), "that it may go well with you and that you may live long in the land." Fathers, do not provoke your children to anger, but bring them up in the discipline and instruction of the Lord.

Proverbs 21:21 ESV

Whoever pursues righteousness and kindness will find life, righteousness, and honor.

Proverbs 3:9 ESV

Honor the LORD with your wealth and with the first fruits of all your produce

HONOR
Psalm 69:6 ESV

Let not those who hope in you be put to shame through me, O Lord GOD of hosts; let not those who seek you be brought to dishonor through me, O God of Israel

SCRIPTURE ON DISHONOR

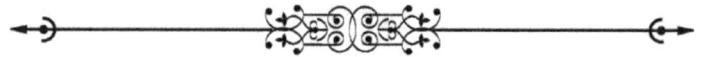

Ezekiel 13:3

'Thus says the Lord GOD, "Woe to the foolish prophets who are following their own spirit and have seen nothing.

Psalm 44:15

All day long my dishonor is before me and my humiliation has overwhelmed me,

Psalm 35:4

Let those be ashamed and dishonored who seek my life; Let those be turned back and humiliated who devise evil against me.

Jeremiah 2:26-28

"As the thief is shamed when he is discovered, So the house of Israel is shamed; They, their kings, their princes and their priests and their prophets, who say to a tree, 'You are my father,' And to a stone, 'You gave me birth.' For they have turned their back to Me, and not their face; But in the time of their trouble they will say, 'Arise and save us.' "But where are your gods Which you made for yourself? Let them arise, if they can save you in the time of your trouble; For according to the number of your cities Are your gods, O Judah

Romans 2:23-24

You who boast in the Law, through your breaking the Law, do you dishonor God? For "THE NAME OF GOD IS BLASPHEMED AMONG THE GENTILES BECAUSE OF YOU," just as it is written.

JANICE WATTS
INTEGRITY

<u>Proverbs 10:9</u> - He that walketh uprightly walketh surely: but he that perverteth his ways shall be known.

<u>Proverbs 28:6</u> - Better [is] the poor that walketh in his uprightness, than [he that is] perverse [in his] ways, though he [be] rich.

<u>Proverbs 11:3</u> - The integrity of the upright shall guide them: but the perverseness of transgressors shall destroy them.

<u>1 John 4:7-10</u> - Beloved, let us love one another: for love is of God; and every one that loveth is born of God, and knoweth God.

<u>Proverbs 19:1</u> - Better [is] the poor that walketh in his integrity, than [he that is] perverse in his lips, and is a fool.

<u>1 Peter 3:16</u> - Having a good conscience; that, whereas they speak evil of you, as of evildoers, they may be ashamed that falsely accuse your good conversation in Christ.

HONOR

Proverbs 20:7 - The just [man] walketh in his integrity: his children [are] blessed after him.

Proverbs 12:22 - Lying lips [are] abomination to the LORD: but they that deal truly [are] his delight.

Colossians 3:23 - And whatsoever ye do, do [it] heartily, as to the Lord, and not unto men;

Luke 16:10 - He that is faithful in that which is least is faithful also in much: and he that is unjust in the least is unjust also in much.

Proverbs 21:3 - To do justice and judgment [is] more acceptable to the LORD than sacrifice.

2 Corinthians 8:21 - Providing for honest things, not only in the sight of the Lord, but also in the sight of men.

Philippians 4:8 - Finally, brethren, whatsoever things are true, whatsoever things [are] honest, whatsoever things [are] just, whatsoever things [are] pure, whatsoever things [are] lovely, whatsoever things [are] of good report; if [there be] any virtue, and if [there be] any praise, think on these things.

About The Author Janice Watts

Janice Watts hails from Houston, Texas. She has been a minister of the gospel for 11 years. She has unique gifting and the Lord has anointed her to speak to the youth of this generation and impact the lives of many across this nation.

Janice facilitates a prophetic training at Lions Roar Prophetic Academy in Belton, Texas at Shiloh Worship Center where she trains and launches prophetic voices in the region.

Moreover her desire is to revival in the people of God while allowing God to use her as a vessel of honor for his glory.

She is also the founder of "Sparkle Girls" created to help the disadvantaged young girls who do not have parental guidance or structure. She partners with KISD and local churches to change this world. She has the heart to impact and change our world.

Contact: wattsministries@gmail.com

HONOR

Honor has become a lost art among the believer many feel they can reach optimum kingdom success without honor., This is in no way possible. When you give dishonor be careful that you don't end up receiving the same. Sow in honor that you may be established in honor.

www.ingramcontent.com/pod-product-compliance
Lightning Source LLC
La Vergne TN
LVHW051849080426
835512LV00018B/3156